JOHN STOTT BIBLE STUDIES

8 Studies with Commentary for Individuals or Groups

The Beatitudes

Developing Spiritual Character

John STOTT

Inter-Varsity Press
Nottingham, England

IVP Connect
An imprint of InterVarsity Press
Downers Grove, Illinois

InterVarsity Press, USA
P.O. Box 1400, Downers Grove, IL 60515-1426, USA
World Wide Web: www.ivpress.com
Email: email@ivpress.com

Inter-Varsity Press, England
Norton Street, Nottingham NG7 3HR, England
Website: www.ivpbooks.com
Email: ivp@ivpbooks.com

InterVarsity Press®, USA, is the book-publishing division of InterVarsity Christian Fellowship/USA®,
a student movement active on campus at hundreds of universities, colleges and schools of nursing in
the United States of America, and a member movement of the International Fellowship of Evangelical
Students. For information about local and regional activities, write Public Relations Dept., InterVarsity
Christian Fellowship/USA, 6400 Schroeder Rd., P.O. Box 7895, Madison, WI 53707-7895, or visit the IVCF
website at <www.intervarsity.org>.

Inter-Varsity Press, England, is closely linked with the Universities and Colleges Christian Fellowship, a
student movement connecting Christian Unions in universities and colleges throughout Great Britain, and
a member movement of the International Fellowship of Evangelical Students. Website: www.uccf.org.uk.

This study guide is based on and includes excerpts from The Message of the Sermon on the Mount ©1978
by John R. W. Stott, originally published under the title Christian Counter-Culture.

Design: Cindy Kiple
Images: malcolm romain/iStockphoto

USA ISBN 978-0-8308-2162-4
UK ISBN 978-1-84474-315-5

Printed in the United States of America ∞

P   23   22   21   20   19   18   17   16   15   14   13   12   11   10   9   8   7   6   5   4   3   2   1

Y   27   26   25   24   23   22   21   20   19   18   17   16   15   14   13   12   11   10   09   08

Introducing the Beatitudes

We seem to have been passing through decades of disillusion. Each rising generation is disaffected with the world it has inherited. Sometimes the reaction has been naive, though that is not to say it has been insincere. The horrors of Vietnam were not brought to an end by those who gave out flowers, saying, "Make love not war," yet their protest did not pass unnoticed. Today the younger generation continues to search for a place they can be at home. They feel alienated by the prevailing culture.

If today's young people are looking for the right things (meaning, love, reality), they are looking for them in the wrong places. The first place they should be able to turn to is the one they normally ignore, the church. For too often what they see in the church is not a new society which embodies their ideals but another version of the old society which they have renounced.

No comment could be more hurtful to the Christian than the words "But you are no different from anybody else." For the essential theme of the whole Bible from beginning to end is that God's historical purpose is to call out a people for himself. This people is a "holy" people, set apart from the world to belong to him and to obey him; its vocation is to be true to its identity, that is, to be "holy" or "different" in all its outlook and behavior.

All this is essential background to the Sermon on the Mount. It describes what human life and human community look like when they come under the gracious rule of God. And what do they look like? Different!

The Context of the Sermon
The Sermon on the Mount is found in Matthew's Gospel toward the beginning of Jesus' public ministry. Immediately after his baptism and temptation he had begun to announce the good news that the kingdom of God, long promised in the Old Testament era, was now on the threshold. It portrays the repentance and the righteousness which belong to the kingdom.

The Sermon is probably the best-known part of the teaching of Jesus. It is also arguably the least understood and certainly the least obeyed. It is Jesus' own description of what he wanted his followers to be and to do. Here is a Christian value-system, ethical standard, religious devotion, attitude to money, ambition, lifestyle and network of relationships—all of which are totally at variance with those of the non-Christian world.

A Message for Us
A majority of readers of the Sermon on the Mount, looking the reality of human perversity in the face, have declared its standards to be unattainable. Its ideals are noble but impractical, they say, attractive to imagine but impossible to fulfill. Others take the superficial approach and glibly assert that the Sermon on the Mount expresses ethical standards which are self-evidently true, common to all religions and easy to follow. One wonders if they have ever read this Sermon which they dismiss as commonplace!

The standards of the Sermon are neither readily attainable by everyone nor totally unattainable by anyone. Jesus spoke this Sermon to those who were already his disciples and thereby also citizens of God's kingdom and the children of God's family. It describes the kind of people reborn Christians are (or should be).

The eight "beatitudes" which begin the Sermon are the focus of this guide. The beatitudes set forth the blessings God gives to those in whom he is working such a character—blessings given not as a reward for merit but as a gift of grace. By working toward the standards Christ has given us and coming as close to the mark as humanly possible, we give evidence of what by God's free grace and gift we already are.

Suggestions for Individual Study

1. As you begin each study, pray that God will speak to you through his Word.

2. Read the introduction to the study and respond to the question that follows it. This is designed to help you get into the theme of the study.

3. The studies are written in an inductive format designed to help you discover for yourself what Scripture is saying. Each study deals with a particular passage so that you can really delve into the author's meaning in that context. Read and reread the passage to be studied. The questions are written using the language of the New International Version, so you may wish to use that version of the Bible. The New Revised Standard Version is also recommended.

4. Each study includes three types of questions. *Observation* questions ask about the basic facts: who, what, when, where and how. *Interpretation* questions delve into the meaning of the passage. *Application* questions (also found in the "Apply" section) help you discover the implications of the text for growing in Christ. These three keys unlock the treasures of Scripture.

Write your answers to the study questions in the spaces provided or in a personal journal. Writing can bring clarity and deeper understanding of yourself and of God's Word.

5. In the studies you will find some commentary notes designed to give help with complex verses by giving further biblical and cultural background and contextual information. The notes in the studies are not designed to answer the questions for you. They are to help you along as you learn to study the Bible for yourself. After you have worked through the questions and notes in the guide, you may want to read the accompanying commentary by John Stott in the Bible Speaks Today series. This will give you more information about the text.

6. Move to the "Apply" section. These questions will help you connect the key biblical themes to your own life. Putting the application into practice is one of the keys to growing in Christ.

7. Use the guidelines in the "Pray" section to focus on God, thanking him for what you have learned and praying about the applications that have come to mind.

Suggestions for Members of a Group Study

1. Come to the study prepared. Follow the suggestions for individual study mentioned above. You will find that careful preparation will greatly enrich your time spent in group discussion.

2. Be willing to participate in the discussion. The leader of your group will not be lecturing. Instead, she or he will be encouraging the members of the group to discuss what they have learned. The leader will be asking the questions that are found in this guide.

3. Stick to the topic being discussed. Your answers should be based on the verses which are the focus of the discussion and not on outside authorities such as commentaries or speakers. These studies focus on a particular passage of Scripture. Only rarely should you refer to other portions of the Bible. This allows for everyone to participate on equal ground and for in-depth study.

4. Be sensitive to the other members of the group. Listen attentively when they describe what they have learned. You may be surprised by their insights! Each question assumes a variety of answers. Many questions do not have "right" answers, particularly questions that aim at meaning or application. Instead the questions push us to explore the passage more thoroughly.

When possible, link what you say to the comments of others. Also, be affirming whenever you can. This will encourage some of the more hesitant members of the group to participate.

5. Be careful not to dominate the discussion. We are sometimes so eager to express our thoughts that we leave too little opportunity for others to respond. By all means participate! But allow others to also.

6. Expect God to teach you through the passage being discussed and through the other members of the group. Pray that you will have an enjoyable and profitable time together, but also that as a result of the study you will find ways that you can take action individually and/or as a group.

7. It will be helpful for groups to follow a few basic guidelines. These guidelines, which you may wish to adapt to your situation, should be read at the beginning of the first session.

☐ Anything said in the group is considered confidential and will not be discussed outside the group unless specific permission is given to do so.

☐ We will provide time for each person present to talk if he or she feels comfortable doing so.

☐ We will talk about ourselves and our own situations, avoiding conversation about other people.

☐ We will listen attentively to each other.

☐ We will be very cautious about giving advice.

8. If you are the group leader, you will find additional suggestions at the back of the guide.

1

PUTTING OUR TRUST IN GOD

Matthew 5:3; Revelation 3:17-22

He only who is reduced to nothing in himself, and relies on the mercy of God, is poor in spirit. (JOHN CALVIN)

Everybody who has ever heard of Jesus of Nazareth and knows anything at all of his teaching must surely be familiar with the "beatitudes" with which the Sermon on the Mount begins. The beatitudes set forth the balanced and variegated character of Christian people. They are Christ's own specification of what every Christian ought to be. Each quality is commended, inasmuch as each person who exhibits it is pronounced "blessed." Just as the eight qualities describe every Christian (at least in the ideal), so the eight blessings are given to every Christian. The first deals with something that doesn't sound much like a blessing to our ears: be "poor in spirit."

Open

■ What are some good things about being poor?

Study

■ Right at the beginning of his Sermon on the Mount, Jesus contradicted all human judgments and all nationalistic expectations of the kingdom of God. The kingdom is given to the poor, not the rich; the feeble, not the mighty; to little children humble enough to accept it, not to soldiers who boast that they can obtain it by their own prowess.

Now when he saw the crowds, he went up on a mountainside and sat down. His disciples came to him, and he began to teach them, saying:

Blessed are the poor in spirit, for theirs is the kingdom of heaven. (Matthew 5:1-3)

---

1. What do verses 1 and 2 tell us about the context of this message and Jesus' listeners?

What do these verses tell us about Jesus?

---

2. How does Jesus' statement in verse 3 contradict our usual idea of blessedness?

Some have translated Jesus' opening words "Happy are . . . " Though the Greek can and does mean "happy," it is seriously misleading to render it "happy" in this case. Happiness is a subjective state, whereas Jesus is making an objective judgment about these people. He is declaring not what they may feel like ("happy"), but what God thinks of them and what on that account they are: they are "blessed."

3. The Old Testament supplies the necessary background against which to interpret this beatitude. At first to be "poor" meant to be in literal, material need. But gradually, because the needy had no refuge but God, "poverty" came to have spiritual overtones. What do you think it means to be "poor in spirit"?

4. Identify some circumstances or insights which have helped you realize that you were "poor in spirit."

5. In your own life how have you been blessed by acknowledging your spiritual poverty?

6. In what senses do we miss God's kingdom if we do not acknowledge our spiritual poverty?

Summary: To be "poor in spirit" is to acknowledge our spiritual bankruptcy before God. For we are sinners, under the holy wrath of God, and deserving nothing but his judgment. We have nothing to offer, nothing to plead, nothing with which to buy the favor of heaven.

The "poor man" in the Old Testament is one who is both afflicted and unable to save himself, and who therefore looks to God for salvation, while recognizing that he has no claim upon God. This kind of spiritual poverty is specially commended in the book of Isaiah.

Perhaps the best example of the way riches can keep us from crying out to God is the nominal church of Laodicea to whom John was directed to send a letter from the glorified Christ. *Read Revelation 3:17-22* for John's assessment of Laodicea.

---

7. How does this assessment of the Laodiceans contradict their own image of themselves (v. 17)?

---

8. It is apparent that the Laodiceans were materially wealthy (v. 17). What other kinds of "wealth" might they have assumed they had accumulated?

This visible church, for all its Christian profession, was not truly Christian at all. Self-satisfied and superficial, it was composed (according to Jesus) of blind and naked beggars. But the tragedy was that they would not admit it. They were rich, not poor, in spirit.

---

9. What sort of spiritual "wealth" do churches today imagine they have accumulated?

10. What remedy did Christ offer the Laodiceans (vv. 18-20)?

11. Verse 20 is often quoted as an invitation for non-Christians to believe in Jesus. But the words were originally spoken to a church. How would Christ's invitation apply to Christians?

12. What did Christ promise as a result of accepting his offer (vv. 21-22)?

13. How do Christ's offer and promise still apply to Christians today?

Summary: The indispensable condition of receiving the kingdom of God is to acknowledge our spiritual poverty. To the poor in spirit, and only to the poor in spirit, the kingdom of God is given. For God's rule which brings salvation is a gift as absolutely free as it is utterly undeserved.

Apply

◼ Sometimes we remain sharply aware of our own failings and dependence on the Lord. In what areas do you readily acknowledge your need of God?

Other times we are like the Laodiceans, oblivious to our own poverty. In what areas do you have trouble acknowledging your neediness?

Pray————————————————

◼ To the Laodiceans Jesus said, "Those whom I love I rebuke and discipline. So be earnest, and repent." Let Jesus speak those words directly to you, and respond to his voice. Pray for a fresh awareness of your spiritual poverty and his generosity. Thank him for making you part of his kingdom.

2
REPENTING OF OUR SINS

Matthew 5:4; Romans 7:21-25

*S*ome Christians seem to imagine that, especially if they are filled with the Holy Spirit, they must wear a perpetual grin and be continuously boisterous and bubbly. However, the Christian life, according to Jesus, is not all joy and laughter. The truth is that there are such things as Christian tears, and too few of us ever weep them. And, as the second beatitude teaches, sorrow can be the source of blessing.

Open
■ When is a time when you feel you have mourned for (that is, grieved or felt sorrow over) something or someone?

Study
■ It is one thing to be spiritually poor and acknowledge it, as the first beatitude says; it is another thing to grieve and to mourn over it. In more

theological language, confession is one thing, contrition is another. One might almost translate the second beatitude "Happy are the unhappy" in order to draw attention to the startling paradox it contains.

> Blessed are those who mourn, for they will be comforted. (Matthew 5:4)

It is plain from the context that those Jesus promised comfort are not primarily those who mourn the loss of a loved one, but those who mourn the loss of their innocence, their righteousness, their self-respect. It is not the sorrow of bereavement to which Christ refers, but the sorrow of repentance.

---

1. What does this beatitude tell you about the heart of God?

---

2. What are some evasions people use to avoid mourning their sins?

---

3. What forms might godly mourning over sin take?

4. What is the difference between self-pity and genuine grieving over sin?

5. How has the Lord comforted you when you have grieved over your sins?

Summary: Jesus wept over the sins of others, over their bitter consequences in judgment and death, and over the impenitent city which would not receive him. We too should weep more over the evil in the world, as did the godly people of biblical times. It is not only the sins of others, however, which should cause us tears; for we have our own sins to weep over as well.

6. Paul was mourning over his own sin when he wrote to the church in Rome. *Read Romans 7:21-25.* What words and phrases throughout this passage highlight the struggle Paul is experiencing?

7. The apostle Paul was chosen by God to spread the gospel through the Roman Empire. He also wrote most of the New Testament. How could he still call himself "wretched" (v. 24)?

8. What was the only solution Paul saw for his wretchedness (vv. 24-25)?

We Christians who make much of grace sometimes thereby make light of sin. There is not enough sorrow for sin among us. We should experience more "godly sorrow" (2 Corinthians 7:10) of Christian penitence.

9. Most of us who are known as Christians are living an outwardly respectable life. Why is it so difficult for us to admit inner sin, either to ourselves or to others?

10. Paul wrote about the inner struggle between God's law and the law of sin at work in his body. How do you empathize with his struggle?

11. In your own life what forms has that "war" taken?

12. In your own life what forms has Christ's "rescue" taken?

Summary: Those who bewail their own sinfulness will be comforted by the only comfort which can relieve their distress, namely the free forgiveness of God. According to the Old Testament prophets, "consolation" was to be one of the offices of the Messiah. Christ does pour oil into our wounds and speak peace to our sore, scarred consciences. Yet still we mourn over the havoc of suffering and death which sin spreads throughout the world. For only in the final state of glory will Christ's comfort be complete, for only then will sin be no more and "God will wipe away every tear from their eyes" (Revelation 7:17).

Apply

■ Think of times you tried to conceal or deny your sins, and then the Lord brought you to the point of repentance. How did you experience mourning over sin?

How did the Lord make his comfort known to you?

Pray

Thank the Lord for his patient pursuit of you and for the undeserved comfort of forgiveness.

Take Paul's statement "Thanks be to God—through Jesus Christ our Lord!" and expand it into your own prayers of thanks: "Thanks be to God through Jesus Christ our Lord for . . . !"

3
LEARNING GENTLENESS

Matthew 5:5; Psalm 37:1-11

I t is comparatively easy to be honest with ourselves before God and acknowledge ourselves to be sinners in his sight, says commentator Martyn Lloyd-Jones. "But," he continues, "how much more difficult it is to allow *other people* to say things like that about me!" (*Studies in the Sermon on the Mount* [Inter-Varsity Press, U.K., 1977], pp. 68-69).

I can read a corporate confession in church and it causes me no great problem; I can take it in stride. But let somebody else come up to me after church and call me a sinner, and I want to punch that person in the nose! I am not prepared to allow other people to think or speak of me what I have just acknowledged before God that I am. There is a basic hypocrisy here; there always is when meekness, the third quality Jesus emphasizes, is absent.

Open
■ Would you want to be called "meek"? Why or why not?

Study

■ Blessed are the meek, for they will inherit the earth. (Matthew 5:5)
The Greek adjective translated "meek," means "gentle," "humble," "considerate," "courteous," and therefore exercising the self-control without which these qualities would be impossible.

---

1. It is important to note that in the beatitudes "the meek" come between those who mourn over sin and those who hunger and thirst after righteousness. The particular form of meekness which Christ requires in his disciples will surely have something to do with this sequence. Compare this beatitude with the preceding two. How is it similar and how is it different?

---

2. What is surprising about this beatitude?

---

3. Why is meekness often looked down on as a character trait?

4. We shrink from the image of Jesus as meek and mild because it conjures up a picture of him as weak and effeminate, yet he described himself as "gentle," using the Greek adjective found in verse 5, and "humble in heart" (Matthew 11:29). How could Jesus be described as a "meek" person?

What sort of gentleness is this, on account of which those who have it are pronounced blessed? I believe Martyn Lloyd-Jones is right to emphasize that this meekness denotes a humble and gentle attitude to others which is determined by a true estimate of ourselves.

5. Think of "gentle," "humble," "considerate" and "courteous" people you have known. Why did you find them admirable?

6. What does it mean to you that the meek will "inherit the earth"?

Rather than the meek inheriting the earth, one would have expected the opposite. One would think that meek people get nowhere because everybody ignores them or else rides roughshod over them and tramples them underfoot. Isn't it the tough, the overbearing who succeed in the struggle for existence? Even the ancient Israelites had to fight for their inheritance, although the Lord their God gave them the Promised Land. But the condition on which we enter our spiritual inheritance in Christ is not might but meekness, for everything is ours if we are Christ's (1 Corinthians 3:22).

Summary: Meekness is a true view of oneself, expressed in attitude and conduct with respect to others. This makes us gentle, humble, sensitive and patient in all our dealings with others.

In Old Testament days, when the wicked seemed to triumph, the holy and humble people of God still had the confidence that they and all things ultimately belonged to God. This confidence was never expressed more aptly than in Psalm 37, which Jesus seems to have been quoting in the beatitudes.

---

7. *Read Psalm 37.* Pick out the verbs in this psalm. How do they express meekness?

---

8. Three times this passage advises us not to fret (vv. 1, 7, 8). How does fretting contradict an attitude of meekness?

---

9. What is the relationship between meekness and trust in God?

10. Which verses in this psalm express the idea that "the meek will inherit the earth"?

11. What promises does this psalm hold for those who continue in an attitude of gentleness and humility?

12. What will be the results of the opposite of meekness—rebelling against the Lord?

13. Which promises in this psalm mean the most to you right now, and why?

Summary: The godless may boast and throw their weight about, yet real possession eludes their grasp. The meek, on the other hand, although they may be deprived and disenfranchised by the world, yet because they know what it is to live and reign with Christ, can enjoy and even "possess" the earth, which belongs to Christ. Then when Christ returns there will be "a new heaven and a new earth" for them to inherit.

Apply ———————————————————————
■ How does your view of "meekness" need to be revised in the light of the character of Christ and this beatitude?

Where do you need to trust God more and not fight for your own way?

Pray ———————————————————————
■ Ask the Lord to show you relationships or situations where you are being proud or harsh instead of gentle and humble. Thank him for setting the example of gentleness in his earthly life and in his continuing dealings with you.

4
BECOMING RIGHTEOUS

Matthew 5:6; Romans 9:30—10:4

For he satisfies the thirsty and fills the hungry with good things. (Psalm 107:9)

Again and again, Scripture addresses its promises to the hungry. Spiritual hunger is the characteristic of all God's people. Our supreme ambition is not material but spiritual. Christians are not like pagans, engrossed in the pursuit of possessions; what they have set themselves to "seek first" is God's kingdom and righteousness (Matthew 6:33). The fourth beatitude deals with our appetite for the things of God.

Open ————————————————————————
■ Why is self-righteousness unattractive?

Study ————————————————————————
■ In the Magnificat Mary said that God "has filled the hungry with good things but has sent the rich away empty" (Luke 1:53). The spiritually poor

and the spiritually hungry were associated, and both were declared blessed. In Jesus' next beatitude this general principle is particularized.

Blessed are those who hunger and thirst for righteousness, for they will be filled. (Matthew 5:6)

---

1. What do you think it means for a person to "hunger and thirst for righteousness"?

---

2. Jesus promises that those with this spiritual hunger will be filled. Having our hunger satisfied is certainly a blessing. In what senses could we be "blessed" even while we continue to hunger and thirst?

---

3. Why does unrighteousness lead to chronic dissatisfaction?

---

4. How do the hunger and thirst for righteousness resemble physical hunger and thirst?

Righteousness in the Bible has at least three aspects: legal, moral and social. Legal righteousness is justification, a right relationship with God. That cannot be Jesus' meaning here, since he was addressing people who had already been made righteous in the legal sense by belonging to him. Moral righteousness is an inner righteousness of heart, mind and motive. But biblical righteousness is more than a private affair; it includes social righteousness as well. Thus Christians are committed to hunger for righteousness in the whole human community as something pleasing to a righteous God.

---

5. Despite Jesus' promise that we will be "filled," why do we continue to hunger and thirst for inner righteousness?

In this life our hunger will never be fully satisfied, nor our thirst fully quenched. Like all the qualities in the beatitudes, hunger and thirst are perpetual characteristics of the disciples of Jesus, as perpetual as poverty of spirit, meekness and mourning. Not till we reach heaven can it be said of us, "Never again will they hunger, never again will they thirst," for only then will Christ our Shepherd lead us to "springs of living water" (Revelation 7:16-17).

---

6. How are you inclined to respond when you see unrighteousness in society? Explain.
☐ Close my eyes   ☐ Feel despair
☐ Get involved in some organized effort
☐ Get involved person-to-person
☐ Other _____

7. In what parts of your life is it easy to see unrighteousness, and in what parts is it difficult?

Summary: There is perhaps no greater secret of progress in Christian living than a healthy, hearty spiritual appetite. If we are conscious of slow spiritual growth, the reason may be that we have a jaded appetite. It is not enough to mourn over past sin; we must also hunger for future righteousness.

When we talk about "pursuing righteousness," we must be cautious about our meaning. According to Paul, the Jews failed to attain righteousness because they were seeking legal righteousness. It was the Gentiles who discovered righteousness—by faith.

8. *Read Romans 9:30—10:4.* Contrast the righteousness of law and the righteousness of faith in Christ.

9. Why is it futile for people to try to establish their own righteousness (10:3)?

10. The righteousness Paul writes about here is "legal righteousness," which those who believe in Jesus have already been given as a gift. In what ways can Christians fall into pursuing righteousness "as if it were by works" (v. 32)?

11. How is the pursuit of righteousness by law different from the "hunger and thirst for righteousness" which Stott says Jesus refers to in Matthew 5:6?

Apply
■ Would you say your "appetite for righteousness" is sharp or dull? Explain.

In what areas of society do you long to see more righteousness?

In what areas of your character do you long to be more righteous?

Pray

■ Praise God that he is perfectly righteous and holy. Ask him to increase your appetite for righteousness both in your own life and in our society. Pray that your life will increasingly reflect God's righteous character.

5
SHOWING MERCY

Matthew 5:7; Matthew 18:21-35

*L*ooking back, we can see that the first four beatitudes reveal a spiritual progression of relentless logic. To begin with, we are to be "poor in spirit," acknowledging our complete and utter spiritual bankruptcy before God. Next we are to "mourn" over the cause of it, our sin, the corruption of our fallen nature and the reign of sin and death in the world. Third, we are to be "meek," humble and gentle toward others, allowing our spiritual poverty to condition our behavior to them as well as to God. And fourth, we are to "hunger and thirst for righteousness," for what is the use of confessing and lamenting our sin, of acknowledging the truth about ourselves to both God and others, if we leave it there?

In the second half of the beatitudes we turn even more from our attitude to God to our attitude to our fellow human beings, beginning with mercy.

Open ──────────────────
■ What have been the effects of mercy in your life?

Study

■ Blessed are the merciful, for they will be shown mercy. (Matthew 5:7)

1. What cause and effect is presented in this beatitude?

2. How have you seen an act of mercy lead to more mercy? Give an example.

"Mercy" is compassion for people in need. Jesus does not specify the categories of people he has in mind to whom his disciples are to show mercy. He gives no indication whether he is thinking primarily of those overcome by disaster, like the traveler from Jerusalem to Jericho whom robbers assaulted and to whom the good Samaritan "had mercy" (Luke 10:30-37), or of the hungry, the sick and the outcast on whom he himself regularly took pity, or of those who wrong us so that justice cries out for punishment but mercy for forgiveness. God's mercy extends to all those people, and so must our mercy.

3. What risks have you taken in showing mercy to others?

4. What risks do you think others have taken in showing mercy to you?

---

5. Many merciful people are treated indifferently or even cruelly in return—Jesus Christ himself being the chief example. How do you reconcile that inescapable fact of life with Jesus' promise in this fifth beatitude?

Of course the world (at least when it is true to its own nature) is unmerciful, as indeed also the church in its worldliness has often been. The world prefers to insulate itself against people's pains and calamities. It finds revenge delicious, and forgiveness, by comparison, tame. But those who show mercy find it.

Summary: Our God is a merciful God and shows mercy continuously; the citizens of his kingdom must show mercy too.

After Jesus gave his disciples what we call "The Lord's Prayer," he said, "For if you forgive men when they sin against you, your heavenly Father will also forgive you" (Matthew 6:14). To forgive and to be forgiven, to show mercy and to receive mercy: these belong indissolubly together, as Jesus illustrated in his parable of the unmerciful servant.

6. *Read Matthew 18:21-35.* What was Peter apparently looking for when he asked his question (v. 21)?

7. What effect would Jesus' answer have had on Peter (v. 22)?

8. In this parable what was the master willing to lose (vv. 23-27)?

9. How did the master display the character of God the Father?

10. How did the servant's behavior reveal his true attitude toward the master's forgiveness (vv. 28-34)?

11. Verse 35 seems cruel and hard to reconcile with a God of love. In what sense does this verse still reflect the character of a merciful God?

The point of this parable is not that we merit mercy by mercy or forgiveness by forgiveness. The point is that we cannot receive the mercy and forgiveness of God unless we repent, and we cannot claim to have repented of our sins if we are unmerciful toward the sins of others. Or, interpreted in the context of the beatitudes, it is "the meek" who are also "the merciful." For to be meek is to acknowledge to others that *we* are sinners; to be merciful is to have compassion on others, for *they* are sinners too.

---

12. How does the outcome of the servant's actions confirm the truth of Jesus' beatitude (vv. 32-35)?

Summary: Nothing moves us to forgive like the wondering knowledge that we ourselves have been forgiven. Nothing proves more clearly that we have been forgiven than our own readiness to forgive.

Apply ─────────────────────────────────
■ What difference has the mercy of other people made in your life?

When are you especially grateful for the mercy of God?

Who can you show mercy to this week?

Pray

■ Taking the mercy of God and the mercy of other people as your example, pray that your life will continually reflect the mercy which has been shown to you. Thank God for his daily mercy which continues toward you even when other people's mercy is imperfect.

6
GROWING
MORE HOLY

Matthew 5:8; Psalm 24:1-6

*H*ow few of us live one life and live it in the open! We are tempted to wear a different mask and play a different role according to each occasion. This is not reality but play-acting, which is the essence of hypocrisy. Some people weave around themselves such a tissue of lies that they can no longer tell which part of them is real and which is make-believe. Alone among all people Jesus Christ was absolutely pure in heart, being entirely guileless.

Open
■ When is it difficult for you to live out in your action what you believe in your heart?

Study
■ In Jesus' first beatitude the words "poor in spirit" indicated the kind of

poverty he meant. In this beatitude the words "in heart" indicate the kind of purity he is alluding to.

Blessed are the pure in heart, for they will see God. (Matthew 5:8)

1. What distinction do you see between being "pure in heart" and being pure in outward behavior?

The popular interpretation of this beatitude is to regard purity of heart as an expression of inward purity, the quality of those who have been cleansed from moral—as opposed to ceremonial—defilement. There is good biblical precedent for this, especially in Psalms. Jesus took up this theme in his controversy with the Pharisees and complained about their obsession with external, ceremonial purity.

2. In what senses will the pure in heart "see God"?

3. How can you tell if a person whose life is outwardly correct is truly "pure in heart"?

4. Think of someone you know whom you would describe as pure in heart. What are the distinguishing marks of that person's life?

This emphasis on the inward and moral, whether contrasted with the outward and ceremonial or with the outward and physical, is certainly consistent with the whole Sermon on the Mount which requires heart-right-eousness rather than mere rule-righteousness. Nevertheless, in the context of the other beatitudes, "purity of heart" seems to refer in some sense to our relationships. It is single-mindedness, having a single heart. More precisely, the primary reference is to sincerity. The pure in heart have their whole lives, public and private, transparent before others. Their very heart—including their thoughts and motives—is pure, unmixed with anything devious, ulterior or base.

5. What are some of the distractions which draw Christians away from singleness of heart?

6. Why is insincerity so destructive to Christian relationships?

7. What does sincerity do for relationships?

Summary: Only the pure in heart will see God, see him now with the eye of faith and see his glory in the hereafter, for only the utterly sincere can bear the dazzling vision in whose light the darkness of deceit must vanish and by whose fire all shams are burned up.

8. *Read Psalm 24* to see how David described a person who is pure in heart. What concepts and word pictures in these verses show what it takes to be worthy before God?

9. How does the fact that everything belongs to God (vv. 1-2) encourage us toward purity of heart?

10. Verse 4 sets forth conditions for coming into God's presence. In your own words, what qualities are called for?

11. For those who live sincerely before God, what outcome is promised (vv. 5-6)?

12. Only Jesus was absolutely pure in heart. Even the ideal person described in Psalm 24 must still be a sinner by nature. What phrases in this psalm give hope that a sinner can still be pure in heart?

13. On what do you rest your hope that you will "see God"?

Summary: The person with "clean hands and a pure heart" is one "who does not lift up his soul to an idol or swear by what is false." (v. 4). This is a person whose relations with both God and other people are free from falsehood.

Apply

■ Consider ways in which you would like your relationships to be purer, that is, more single-minded and sincere. What risks are involved?

What would make the risks worth it?

Pray

■ Thank the Lord for being the perfect example of purity of heart. Ask him to show you areas where you have mixed motives or any hypocrisy. Pray for greater sincerity and singleness of heart before him and others.

7
MAKING PEACE

Matthew 5:9; Ephesians 2:11-22

*O*ne of the most frequent causes of conflict is intrigue, while openness and sincerity are essential to all true reconciliation. It is the devil who is a troublemaker; it is God who loves reconciliation and who now through his children, as formerly through his only begotten Son, is bent on making peace. Every Christian, according to Jesus, is meant to be a peacemaker both in the community and in the church. Thus, the sequence of thought from purity of heart in verse 8 to peacemaking in verse 9 is natural.

Open ───────────────────────────────

■ When have you found yourself in the role of peacemaker?

Study ───────────────────────────────

■ Some time after the Sermon on the Mount, Jesus was to say that "I did not come to bring peace, but a sword" (Matthew 10:34). What he meant was that conflict would be the inevitable result of his coming, even in one's own family, and that if we are to be worthy of him, we must love him best and put him first. It is clear beyond question throughout the teaching of Jesus and his apostles, however, that we should never seek out conflict or be responsible for it. On the contrary, we are called to peace, we are to actively "seek peace and pursue it" (1 Peter 3:11), we are to "make every effort to live in peace with all men" (Hebrews 12:14), and so far as it depends on us, we are to "live at peace with everyone" (Romans 12:18).

Blessed are the peacemakers, for they will be called sons of God. (Matthew 5:9)

---

1. What are some characteristics of a person who is a peacemaker?

---

2. Why would peacemakers be recognized as children of God?

---

3. What is the difference between being a peacemaker and being conciliatory?

The words *peace* and *appeasement* are not synonyms. For the peace of God is not peace at any price. He made peace with us at immense cost, even at the price of the life-blood of his only Son. We too—though in lesser ways—will find peacemaking a costly enterprise. To proclaim "peace, peace" where there is no peace is the work of the false prophet, not the Christian witness (Jeremiah 6:14; 8:11). When we ourselves are involved in a quarrel, there will be either the pain of apologizing to the person we have injured or the pain of rebuking the person who has injured us.

4. What are some of the costs of being a peacemaker?

5. What are some of the rewards of peacemaking?

Summary: Peacemaking is a divine work. For peace means reconciliation, and God is the author of peace and of reconciliation. True peace and true forgiveness are costly treasures.

The same verb which is used in this beatitude of us is applied by the apostle Paul to what God has done through Christ. Through Christ God was pleased "to reconcile to himself all things . . . *making peace* through his blood, shed on the cross" (Colossians 1:20). Christ's purpose was to "create in himself one new man out of the two [Jew and Gentile], thus *making peace*" (Ephesians 2:15). *Read Ephesians 2:11-22* to better understand our role as peacemakers.

7. What was the chronic conflict between Jew and Gentile (vv. 11-12)?

8. How did Christ reconcile the conflict (vv. 13-17)?

9. What are the benefits of Christ's peacemaking (vv. 18-22)?

10. How was this reconciliation a costly one?

11. When have you observed conflicts in church between "insiders" and "outsiders"?

12. All Christians, no matter what their ethnic background, have "access to the Father by one Spirit" (v. 18). How can this truth promote peace among Christians who have natural differences, even antagonisms?

Even if we are not personally involved in a dispute, we may find ourselves struggling to reconcile to each other two people or groups who are estranged and at variance with each other. In this case there will be the pain of listening, of ridding ourselves of prejudice, or of striving sympathetically to understand both the opposing points of view, and of risking misunderstanding, ingratitude or failure.

Summary: Jesus prayed for the oneness of his people; he also prayed that they might be kept from evil and in truth (John 17). We have no mandate from Christ to seek unity without purity of both doctrine and conduct.

Apply —————————————————————————

■ Consider each of the parts of your life listed below. Where do you see the need for reconciliation, and what steps will you take to be a peacemaker in those situations?

Category	Need for Reconciliation	Steps to Peace
Relationships		
Family		
Church		

Community

World

In which of these areas you've noted do you feel called to begin working and praying for peace?

Pray————————————————————————————
■ Give praise to Christ for dying for you and reconciling you to God. Pray for his guidance in the steps you should take to become a peacemaker or to continue a peacemaking process. Ask for wisdom so that you will neither shrink from the risks nor go the easy route of appeasement.

8
REJOICING THROUGH PERSECUTION

Matthew 5:10-12; Acts 5:17-42

*H*owever hard we may try to make peace with some people, they refuse to live at peace with us. Not all attempts at reconciliation succeed. Indeed, some take the initiative to oppose us, and in particular to slander us, not because of our foibles or idiosyncrasies, but "because of righteousness" and "because of me" (Matthew 5:10-11). Persecution is simply the clash between two irreconcilable value systems. Thus, Jesus moves from peacemaking to persecution as the final topic of his Sermon.

Open —————————————————————

■ Think of a time when you experienced insults because of Christ. How did you respond?

Study

■ How did Jesus expect his disciples to react under persecution? We are not to retaliate like an unbeliever, nor to sulk like a child, nor to lick our wounds in self-pity like a dog, nor just to grin and bear it like a Stoic, still less to pretend we enjoy it like a masochist. Instead we are to "Rejoice and be glad"!

Blessed are those who are persecuted because of righteousness,
    for theirs is the kingdom of heaven.
Blessed are you when people insult you, persecute you and falsely say all kinds of evil against you because of me. Rejoice and be glad, because great is your reward in heaven, for in the same way they persecuted the prophets who were before you. (Matthew 5:10-12)

---

1. What examples of types of persecution are mentioned here?

---

2. Which of those types of persecution have you experienced?

---

3. What forms of persecution do you see active in your own community?

4. What is the most subtle form of persecution you have experienced or seen aimed at other Christians?

Since all the beatitudes describe what every Christian disciple is intended to be, we conclude that the condition of being despised and rejected, slandered and persecuted, is as much a normal mark of Christian discipleship as being pure in heart or merciful. Every Christian is to be a peacemaker, and every Christian is to expect opposition. Those who hunger for righteousness will suffer for the righteousness they crave. We should not be surprised if anti-Christian hostility increases, but rather be surprised if it does not.

5. Verse 12 points to our "reward in heaven," a cause for joy in the midst of persecution. In contrast to rejoicing, what are our more natural reactions to persecution?

6. What reasons does Jesus give us to rejoice when we are persecuted?

7. Identify some differences between being persecuted for the sake of Christ and simply drawing fire for being obnoxious.

Summary: When we undergo persecution we are to rejoice as a Christian should rejoice and even to "leap for joy" (Luke 6:23). Why? Partly because "great is your reward in heaven." We may lose everything on earth, but we shall inherit everything in heaven, not as a reward for merit, but freely. We also rejoice partly because persecution is a token of genuineness, a certificate of Christian authenticity, since the prophets before us were persecuted. But the major reason why we should rejoice is because we are suffering "because of me," (v. 11), on account of our loyalty to Jesus and to his standards of truth and righteousness.

In Acts 5:17-42 we see the apostles putting this teaching into practice. Having been beaten and threatened by the Sanhedrin, they left "rejoicing because they had been counted worthy of suffering disgrace for the Name" (v. 41).

8. *Read Acts 5:17-42.* This event happened in Jerusalem very early in the life of the Christian church, even before the conversion of Paul. The church was meeting publicly and attracting more followers, which stirred up the jealousy of the Jewish religious leaders. What attempts did they make to silence the apostles (vv. 18, 26-28, 33, 40)?

9. What evidences do you see that God's sovereignty upheld and protected the apostles (vv. 19-20, 34-40)?

10. In spite of the fact that God was with them, how did the apostles suffer (vv. 18, 27, 40)?

11. Looking back through the whole passage, in what ways do the disciples embody the character qualities in the beatitudes?

Character Quality   **Disciples' Actions**

Poor in spirit

Mourn (their sin)

Meek

Hunger for righteousness

Merciful

Pure in heart

Peacemakers

Persecuted for righteousness

_____

12. How are those who are persecuted in this passage also blessed (vv. 41-42)?

Summary: The world considers those "blessed" who are secure and popular and live at ease, not those who have to suffer persecution. The Christian cannot expect to be thanked for being merciful or sincere or a peacemaker; instead we are opposed, slandered, insulted and persecuted on account of the righteousness for which we stand and the Christ with whom we are identified. Such is the man or woman who is "blessed," that is, who has the approval of God and finds self-fulfillment as a human being.

Apply —————————————————————————
■ Consider ways that you have attracted insults on account of your Christian faith. Is it possible that any of those insults were for some other reason than Christ himself? Explain.

_____

What is your usual attitude under persecution?

Look back over the list of character qualities (in question 11) that we have studied. How might growing in one of these areas help you to be ready to face persecution?

Pray————————————————————————

■ With the first-century apostles, rejoice in the Lord's presence that he considers you "worthy of suffering disgrace for the Name." If your attitude under persecution is something other than rejoicing, pray for a clearer understanding of your blessedness.

Guidelines for Leaders

My grace is sufficient for you. (2 Corinthians 12:9)

If leading a small group is something new for you, don't worry. These sessions are designed to be led easily. Because the Bible study questions flow from observation to interpretation to application, you may feel as if the studies lead themselves.

You don't need to be an expert on the Bible or a trained teacher to lead a small group discussion. As a leader, you can guide group members to discover for themselves what the Bible has to say and to listen for God's guidance. This method of learning will allow group members to remember much more of what is said than a lecture would.

This study guide is flexible. You can use it with a variety of groups—students, professionals, neighborhood or church groups. Each study takes forty-five to sixty minutes in a group setting.

There are some important facts to know about group dynamics and encouraging discussion. The suggestions listed below should equip you to effectively and enjoyably fulfill your role as leader.

Preparing for the Study

1. Ask God to help you understand and apply the passage in your own life. Unless this happens, you will not be prepared to lead others. Pray too for the various members of the group. Ask God to open your hearts to the message of his Word and motivate you to action.

2. Read the introduction to the entire guide to get an overview of the topics that will be explored.

3. As you begin each study, read and reread the assigned Bible passage to familiarize yourself with it.

4. This study guide is based on the New International Version of the Bible. It will help you and the group if you use this translation as the basis for your study and discussion.

5. Carefully work through each question in the study. Spend time in meditation and reflection as you consider how to respond.

6. Write your thoughts and responses in the space provided in the study guide. This will help you to express your understanding of the passage clearly.

7. You may want to get a copy of the Bible Speaks Today commentary by John Stott that supplements the Bible book you are studying. The commentary is divided into short units on each section of Scripture so you can easily read the appropriate material each week. This will help you answer tough questions about the passage and its context.

It may help to have a Bible dictionary handy. Use it to look up any unfamiliar words, names or places. (For additional help on how to study a passage, see *How to Lead a LifeGuide Bible Study* from InterVarsity Press, USA.)

8. Take the "Apply" portion of each study seriously. Consider how you need to apply the Scripture to your life. Remember that the group members will follow your lead in responding to the studies. They will not go any deeper than you do.

Leading the Study

1. Begin the study on time. Open with prayer, asking God to help the group to understand and apply the passage.

2. Be sure that everyone in your group has a study guide. Encourage the group to prepare beforehand for each discussion by reading the introduction to the guide and by working through the questions in each study.

3. At the beginning of your first time together, explain that these studies are meant to be discussions, not lectures. Encourage the members of the group to participate. However, do not put pressure on those who may be hesitant to speak during the first few sessions.

4. Have a group member read aloud the introduction at the beginning of the discussion.

5. Every session begins with an "open" question, which is meant to be asked before the passage is read. These questions are designed to introduce the theme of the study and encourage group members to begin to open up. Encourage as many members as possible to participate, and be ready to get the discussion going with your own response.

These opening questions can reveal where our thoughts or feelings need to be transformed by Scripture. That is why it is especially important not to read the passage before the question is asked. The passage will tend to color the honest reactions people would otherwise give because they are, of course, supposed to think the way the Bible does.

6. Have a group member read aloud the passage to be studied.

7. As you ask the study questions, keep in mind that they are designed to be used just as they are written. You may simply read them aloud. Or you may prefer to express them in your own words.

There may be times when it is appropriate to deviate from the study guide. For example, a question may have already been answered. If so, move on to the next question. Or someone may raise an important question not covered in the guide. Take time to discuss it, but try to keep the group from going off on tangents.

8. Avoid answering your own questions. If necessary repeat or rephrase them until they are clearly understood. Or point the group to the commentary woven into the guide to clarify the context or meaning without answering the question. An eager group quickly becomes passive and silent if members think the leader will do most of the talking.

9. Don't be afraid of silence in response to the discussion questions. People may need time to think about the question before formulating their answers.

10. Don't be content with just one answer. Ask, "What do the rest of you think?" or "Anything else?" until several people have given answers to the question.

11. Acknowledge all contributions. Try to be affirming whenever possible. Never reject an answer. If it is clearly off-base, ask, "Which verse led you to that conclusion?" or again, "What do the rest of you think?"

12. Don't expect every answer to be addressed to you, even though this will probably happen at first. As group members become more at ease, they will begin to truly interact with each other. This is one sign of healthy discussion.

13. Don't be afraid of controversy. It can be very stimulating. If you don't resolve an issue completely, don't be frustrated. Explain that the group will move on and God may enlighten all of you in later sessions.

14. Periodically summarize what the group has said about the passage. This helps to draw together the various ideas mentioned and gives continuity to the study. But don't preach.

15. Conclude your time together with conversational prayer, adapting the prayer suggestion at the end of the study to your group. Ask for God's help in following through on the commitments you've made.

16. End on time.

Many more suggestions and helps can be found in *How to Lead a LifeGuide Bible Study* and *The Big Book on Small Groups* (both from InterVarsity Press, USA) or *Housegroups* (Crossway Books, UK). Reading through one of these books would be worth your time.